Her Majesty, Queen Elizabeth,
The Queen Mother
❧ 90 Glorious Years ❧

Researched and written by *Laurence Anthony*. Edited by *Kesta Desmond*. Layout and design by *Louise Ivimy*. Cover photograph supplied by *Photographers International*. All inside photographs supplied by *Syndication International*.

Published by

GRANDREAMS LIMITED
Jadwin House,
205/211 Kentish Town Road,
London NW5 2JU.

Printed in Belgium.

ISBN 0 86227 796 5.

Contents

Childhood Days

On Saturday August 4, 1900, a daughter was born to Lord and Lady Glamis. Seven weeks later the child was christened in the parish church of St. Paul's Walden Bury, in Hertfordshire. She was given the name Lady Elizabeth Angela Margurite Bowes-Lyon.

Although her birth certificate gives her birthplace as St. Paul's Walden Bury, where her parents owned a country home, Lady Elizabeth was in fact born at their London home, 20 St. James's Square. The error was made by Lord Glamis when he registered his daughter's birth in Hitchin.

At the time of the birth Queen Victoria still reigned over the British Empire. And the citizens of that empire were looking forward with eager enthusiasm to the bright future promised by the brand new twentieth century.

Those were the days before the motor car became the popular mode of transport ... Before radio was a means of mass communication ... Before manned flight was possible. They were also the halcyon days before the two World Wars which would alter the face of Great Britain forever.

Although no-one would have dreamed it at the time, the newly-born Lady Elizabeth was destined to become one of the most popular members of the British Royal Family.

The ancestry of Lady Elizabeth Bowes-Lyon is firmly rooted in the history of Scotland. Indeed, it dates back to the late 1300's when Scotland was ruled by Robert II, grandson of the renowned Robert the Bruce.

The King's Chamberlain was one Sir John Lyon - known as 'The White Lyon' thanks to his shock of fair hair. He married the King's daughter, Princess Jean.

The marriage settlement included Sir John being made Thane of Glamis and owner of Glamis Castle. And it is from this marriage that Lady Elizabeth is directly descended.

The Earldom of Strathmore and Kingshorne was bestowed on the family in the Stuart era.

In the eighteenth century the 19th Lord Glamis married one Eleanor Bowes, the daughter of a wealthy industrialist and Member of Parliament, who transferred his fortune and his estates to the Lyon family on condition that they change their name to Bowes! This they did, but later re-adopted their original name and eventually settled on 'Bowes-Lyon'.

Lady Elizabeth's father was Claude George Bowes-Lyon, Lord Glamis. He was also Lord Lieutenant of Angus and was considered a quiet, hard working fellow.

Her mother was the former Cecilia Cavendish-Bentinck, a grand-daughter of the Fourth Earl of Portland, a lady of outgoing character and a leading light of the social scene.

The couple had married on July 16, 1881, in Petersham, Hampshire.

The young Elizabeth was the ninth child and fourth daughter born to Lord and Lady Glamis. Their first girl, Violet, had been born eighteen years earlier, in 1882, but was to die of diphtheria at the age of 11.

Then came Mary Frances, born in 1883; Patrick, in 1884; John Herbert, in 1886; Alexander Francis, in 1887; Fergus, in 1889; Rose Constance, in 1890 and Michael Claude, in 1893.

A sixth son, David, was born in 1902, two years after Elizabeth's birth. The two youngest children would become very close to one another and were nicknamed 'the two Benjamins' by their mother.

To accommodate such a large family as well as the staff necessary to serve them, the beautiful Queen Anne mansion

Lady Elizabeth Bowes-Lyon at the age of 7.

at St. Paul's Walden Bury had to be extended. A new wing was added and it was there that the young Elizabeth received her first education.

She and David were cared for by Clara Knight, their nanny, known affectionately as 'Alla' - a faithful servant who would remain a close friend to the family for the rest of her life.

The baby Elizabeth was a happy child who was early to walk and to talk. She loved her Hertfordshire home, with its ample, well laid-out gardens dotted with statues and woodland. Inside, there were intriguing corridors to explore.

There were pets too. A Shetland pony called 'Bobs', as well as numerous dogs and cats and tortoises.

She also loved Glamis Castle, inherited by her father when he became the 14th Earl of Strathmore in February 1904, on the death of his father. The family, servants, pets and all would travel northwards on the famous train, the 'Flying Scotsman', to spend lengthy holidays there.

Glamis Castle was steeped in history and legend. Ghosts were said to roam the cold stone stairways, among them 'The Grey Lady', 'Old Beardie' and 'Jack the Runner'.

And stories abounded about the ancient castle's place in Scottish history. Bonnie Prince Charlie once stayed there, as did the famous Victorian author, Sir Walter Scott. William Shakespeare is reputed to have dreamed up the plot of MacBeth during a visit to Glamis.

The young Elizabeth took all this in and often acted as a kind of unofficial guide, showing distinguished visitors around the castle. One such guest was Lady Scott, wife of the famous Antarctic explorer Robert Falcon Scott.

As the holidays progressed, the younger children would continue their education under the watchful eye of 'Alla'. They would enjoy picnics and games in the castle grounds. And there would be musical evenings in the Great Hall, in the glow of a welcoming log fire.

They also stayed at Streatlam Castle, the home of the Bowes line of the family, in County Durham.

There was the London residence too, at No. 20, St. James's Square where lady Elizabeth had been born. This was invariably their base during the 'season', throughout which members of high society enjoyed a whirl of parties and social gatherings.

During the 1905 season the five-year-old Lady Elizabeth attended a children's party at which she met, for the first time, Prince Albert, a grandson of King Edward VII (who had succeeded Queen Victoria on her death in 1901).

Neither child could possibly have foreseen that their destinies were inextricably linked.

Left: *Lady Elizabeth Bowes-Lyon, aged 9, mounted on her Shetland pony 'Bobs'.*
Above: *The young Prince Albert waiting on wounded soldiers at Buckingham Palace.*

The Young Lady Elizabeth

Lady Elizabeth's education had been broadened by the introduction of a French governess and later a German governess. She learned drawing, dancing and music and she was a devout churchgoer.

She grew into an extremely pleasant and likeable young woman, with bright, violet-blue eyes and a rosy complexion.

She was a happy and sociable girl, considered to be mature and sensible beyond her years.

As the young Elizabeth blossomed into womanhood, history was changing around her. King Edward VII died in May 1910 and was succeeded by his second son, George V.

Later that summer, the ten-year-old Lady Elizabeth visited a fortune-teller's tent during a garden party at Glamis Castle. It is said that the gypsy foretold that she would one day become a Queen. The young girl dismissed the notion as nonsense, saying, "Who wants to be a Queen anyway!"

Four years later, on August 4, 1914 (Elizabeth's fourteenth birthday), Britain declared war on Germany and the so-called 'Great War' began. It was popularly believed that the conflict would be "all over by Christmas". But in fact the war was to rage for the next four years.

Four of Lady Elizabeth's older brothers went off to war - Patrick, John and Fergus joined the Black Watch, while Michael enlisted in the Royal Scots Regiment. Her sister, Lady Rose, trained to become a nurse.

A week after the declaration of war Lady Elizabeth and her mother travelled north to Glamis Castle, which was to be used as a convalescent hospital for wounded servicemen.

Within a matter of weeks the place was a hive of activity with Red Cross volunteers helping in the conversion. Lady Elizabeth was closely involved too, running errands whenever asked, sewing shirts for the local regiment, knitting, and crumpling up tissue paper for use as insulation in sleeping bags.

The work was interrupted in September 1914 when the family gathered to celebrate the weddings of Fergus to Lady Christian Dawson-Damer on the 17th, and of John to Fenella Hepburn-Stuart-Forbes-Trefusis on the 29th.

Then it was back to work at Glamis.

The wounded began to arrive shortly before Christmas. Known as 'the boys in blue' they had been treated in the Dundee Royal Infirmary and were to recuperate at Glamis. They were all welcomed by Elizabeth's mother, Lady Strathmore.

In 1915 Lady Rose - by then a fully trained nurse - arrived at the castle/hospital to take charge of things.

Elizabeth was eager to help but was considered too young for the work.

However, while her education continued under a new English governess, Lady Elizabeth was to become an important and popular member of the hospital administration.

Her main duty was the collection of the mail and its distribution among the patients. She remembered all their names and also ran errands for them, helped them to write letters home, played the piano and sang to them, played cards

with them, took meals with them - in short, her presence helped to keep up morale in the hospital.

Tragedy struck the family in September 1915 when they suffered the loss of Fergus in the Battle of Loos only the day after he had returned from leave.

Events took a happier turn just nine months later in May 1916, when Lady Elizabeth was bridesmaid at Lady Rose's wedding. She married Naval Commander, William Spencer Levenson Gower, in London.

With her sister gone from Glamis, and her mother still greatly distressed by the loss of Fergus, the teenage Elizabeth assumed more responsibility and took to personally welcoming new patients at the hospital.

On a Saturday evening in the autumn of 1916, Lady Elizabeth spotted a pall of smoke coming from high up in the central keep of the castle. She quickly telephoned for the local fire brigade. Then she called the Dundee brigade before organising the castle staff into a makeshift chain of buckets and bowls.

In the event, the calling of the Dundee brigade actually saved the castle and many of its treasures, as the equipment of the local fire fighting force was unable to cope with the emergency.

The family received more bad news in 1917 when the War Office informed them that their son, Michael, was reported missing in action. Elizabeth's brother, David, refused to believe the report and he refused to wear mourning clothes. Indeed, it later transpired that Michael was still alive, a prisoner-of-war in Germany (he eventually came home in 1919).

The First World War ended on November 11, 1918. But the hospital work at Glamis continued well into the following year. In all, around 1,500 wounded servicemen had convalesced at the castle throughout the war.

Many of them would remember the young Lady Elizabeth with fondness.

Grandchildren

Opposite page, top: *The Duke & Duchess of York*, opposite page, bottom: *Prince Edward*, above: *The Princess Royal* and right: *Prince Charles*.

The Duke & Duchess of York (George VI & Queen Elizabeth) at a house party in 1925.

The Duke of York and his bride, Lady Elizabeth Bowes-Lyon at Buckingham Palace.

*L*ady Elizabeth was an attractive young woman of eighteen when the war ended and the events of the past four years had shown her to be an extremely responsible and capable person.

Gradually her life returned to normal and like most highborn girls she was given a 'coming out' dance by her parents. She was ill and running a temperature on the day of the dance, but insisted that it go ahead in order not to disappoint her friends and family.

There were other parties, too, and in July 1919 her first days at the races, an interest that would occupy much of her time in later years.

Among Lady Elizabeth's friends was Princess Mary, daughter of King George V. In 1920 she was invited to Buckingham Palace where she met the King and Queen Mary. She also met again Prince Albert, Duke of York.

Known as 'Bertie' to the family, Prince Albert had been born on December 14, 1895. As a child he had suffered ill health. For a while his legs had been kept in splints in an effort to straighten them. He was naturally left-handed, but his father insisted that he write with his right hand. He also developed a noticeable stammer.

'Bertie' was a shy boy who had lived his life in the shadow of his older brother Edward, Prince of Wales - a charming, good-looking fellow who was being groomed for future kingship.

Yet for all that, Prince Albert had grown into a sturdy young man with a mind of his own. He had been a Naval officer during the war and was a veteran of the Battle of Jutland. He was also a qualified RAF pilot, an accomplished tennis player and a Cambridge graduate.

The boy Lady Elizabeth had first met at a children's party in 1905 was now a young man of twenty-five. And, like several other young men of the time, he was smitten by Lady Elizabeth Bowes- Lyon.

For the next two years the persistent Prince wooed the girl of his dreams. When he told his father, in 1921, that he intended to ask Lady Elizabeth to become his wife, the King replied that he'd be "a lucky fellow if she accepts you!"

Indeed, Lady Elizabeth was rather hesitant about taking the giant step out of the relative privacy of her own happy circle and into the glare of the public eye, under which the royal family lived. She had not, after all, been trained for the rigid routine of royalty.

However, on Saturday, January 13, 1923, while she and the Prince strolled through the gardens at St. Paul's Walden Bury, she finally accepted the engagement. Three days later a Court Circular announced the news to the nation at large. Suddenly, the name of Elizabeth Bowes-Lyon was on everyone's lips.

The wedding took place at Westminster Abbey on Thursday April 26. The twenty-two year-old bride wore a dress of deep ivory which had been made to blend with a train of antique lace presented by Queen Mary.

It was a rainy morning, but as the King himself wrote 'the sun actually came out as the bride entered the Abbey'.

In a spontaneous and much appreciated

The Duke & Duchess of York on an aerial railway at the Wembley Exhibition June 27, 1925.

On honeymoon at Polesden Lacey (1923).

gesture she then placed her bouquet - of York roses and Scottish heather - on the tomb of the Unknown Warrior, before proceeding along the aisle.

The service was conducted by the Archbishop of Canterbury while the Duke's brother, Edward, Prince of Wales was best man. Afterwards, the newlyweds rode in a royal coach to Buckingham Palace and were greeted by cheering crowds along every inch of the way.

Lady Elizabeth was now Her Royal Highness Princess Elizabeth, The Duchess of York, and her life would be changed forever.

The happy couple spent the first part of their honeymoon at Polesden Lacey, near Great Bookham, in Surrey, having travelled there by train from Waterloo Station.

Later they moved north of the border to Glamis Castle. Unfortunately the new Princess developed a decidedly unromantic bout of whooping cough there!

After the honeymoon the young couple settled temporarily into Frogmore House in the grounds of Windsor Castle.

Meanwhile, their new home - White Lodge in Richmond Park - was being made ready for their occupation.

The Duchess began to undertake public engagements and became patron to several worthy organisations. She took to these tasks with ease, and with her characteristic energy and warmth.

She fitted in well with the royal family and was well liked by the King and Queen and by her brother-in-law, the Prince of Wales. Her role in life seemed well defined.

But fate had other plans in store.

Royal _Births_

At 2.40 am, on April 21, 1926, the Duke and Duchess of York became the proud parents of a baby daughter. She was born at No.17 Bruton Street (the London home of the Duchess's parents since 1920).

On May 29, in a ceremony conducted by the Archbishop of Canterbury and held in the private chapel at Buckingham Palace, the child was christened Elizabeth Alexandra Mary. She was third in line to the throne of England, after her Uncle Edward and her father.

Eight months later, on the instruction of King George V, the Duke and Duchess left England on board the battleship HMS Renown, for an official tour of Australia and New Zealand. Among their duties on the tour was the opening of the new parliament building in the Australian capital, Canberra.

They were unable to take their baby, Princess Elizabeth, but left her in the capable care of the ever-faithful 'Alla'. Throughout the trip the devoted nanny sent them snapshots and progress reports so that they could keep up with the development of their child.

The tour proved an undoubted success, particularly for the Duchess who

Above: The King and Queen, Duke and Duchess of York, Duke of Connaught, Princess Mary and the Earl and Countess of Strathmore at the christening of Princess Elizabeth.

Left: Their first daughter, Elizabeth.

Coming ashore after the Australian and New Zealand tour.

made many new friends and was accepted wherever she went.

On the North Island of New Zealand she met again some of the men who had convalesced at Glamis Castle during the war. She was as pleased to see them as they were to see her.

Back in London, six months later, the royal couple moved into a magnificent new home - No.145 Piccadilly.

The Duchess of York gave birth to her second child, at Glamis Castle, on August 21, 1930. The Duke and Duchess had been convinced that this child would be a boy and had thought up several male names to choose from.

Contrary to expectations, however, the new arrival turned out to be a girl.

After discussions within the family the baby was named Margaret Rose.

The four-year-old Princess Elizabeth was delighted. "I've got a baby sister, Margaret Rose," she said. "And I'm going to call her 'Bud' ... She's not a real rose yet, is she? Only a bud!"

In the autumn of 1931, King George presented the Duke and Duchess of York with The Royal Lodge, in Windsor Great Park. It was a fine house which had fallen into disrepair. But the royal couple were determined to restore it to former glory.

The work took a year to complete - but after that The Royal Lodge became the family's favourite home and they would often spend weekends there.

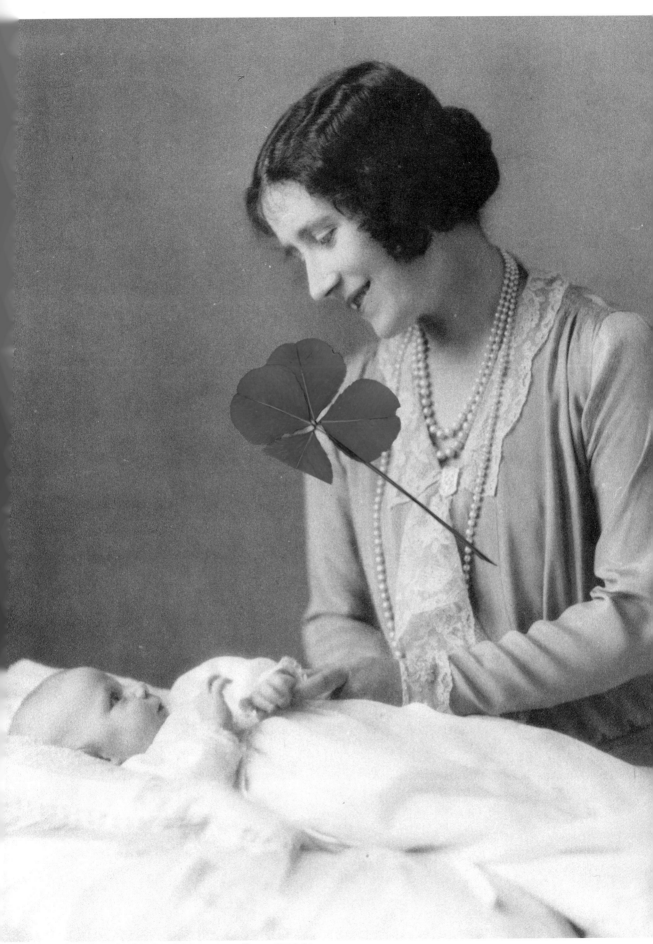

Shortly after the birth of Margaret Rose (1930).

The Queen and Prince Philip with
Prince Charles, Princess Anne and
Prince Andrew.

Turmoil & Change

King George V died at Sandringham on January 20, 1936, and his eldest son, the Prince of Wales, acceded to the throne as King Edward VIII.

But the reign was to be a short one.

Edward was now forty-one years-old and still a bachelor - obviously the most eligible bachelor in the land. This fact had rankled with King George and Queen Mary who had seen each of their younger sons married.

In fact, Edward had for some time been in love with an American woman two years older than himself. Her name was Wallis Simpson and he wanted to marry her. This seemingly simple proposition caused a major constitutional crisis that was to reverberate around the world.

For many weeks arguments raged behind the scenes - and out of the public eye - as to whether the King of England should marry a woman who was not only a commoner, but had also been divorced.

The situation was finally resolved on Thursday December 10, when the King announced that he would abdicate in order to marry Mrs Simpson. His reign had lasted for less than eleven months.

Two days later, Prince Albert acceded to the throne, as King George VI. It was a truly momentous event which was to bring about the greatest upheaval in the lives of the royal couple and their daughters.

Although it had always been a possibility, they had hardly expected the highest honour in the land to be thrust upon them in such a sudden manner.

The news came as a great shock to the public too. After all, there had not been an abdication in England for over 500 years. Now, many people felt that the

THE DAILY MIRROR, Thursday, December 10, 1936

Daily Mirror

No. 10305   Registered at the G.P.O. as a newspaper   ONE PENNY

LONDON·ED

THE KING DECIDES: ABDICATION PLANS

DRAMATIC VISIT TO QUEEN MARY

THE KING HAS DECIDED.

His abdication—unless he makes an eleventh hour change in his decision—is regarded by the Cabinet as imminent.

His Majesty's decision will be announced by Mr. Baldwin in the House of Commons this afternoon. Lord Halifax will make a similar statement in the House of Lords.

Last night the Labour and Liberal Opposition leaders were informed by the Government of the latest moves in the crisis, and advised that there is little hope of a happy solution.

YESTERDAY AFTERNOON THE KING SLIPPED SECRETLY OUT OF FORT BELVEDERE—THE FIRST TIME HE HAD LEFT THE FORT FOR SIX DAYS—AND HE DROVE TO WINDSOR GREAT PARK, WHERE, IN ROYAL LODGE, HE HAD TEA WITH HIS MOTHER, QUEEN MARY.

This meeting was of the most moving character and had been arranged with the utmost privacy.

Elaborate precautions were taken to enable King Edward to leave the Fort unobserved.

Over Rough-Track Roads

To avoid being seen, the King left by one of the rough track roads seldom used by cars and was able to make the two-mile journey without being seen.

His car had only to traverse 200 yards of public roadway before it crossed from his estate into the long private drive through Windsor Great Park to the Lodge.

No one working in the grounds was allowed to see the King leave the house. Workmen were told to remain hidden in a garage.

After spending half an hour with his mother the King returned as secretly to the Fort.

Queen Mary was accompanied by the Princess Royal and the Earl of Athlone Later she dined with the Duke and Duchess of Kent.

In Mr. Baldwin's private room at the House of Commons last night a special Cabinet meeting was called and Ministers were frankly told of all developments.

The King had a further consultation with his brothers, the Duke of York and the Duke of Kent at Fort Belvedere during the day. The Duke of York did not return to London till 9 p.m. He looked pale and worn. In the event of abdication he will automatically succeed to the Crown.

Throughout the day dispatch riders with important messages from London had arrived at the Fort. The King's car drove out at 8.30 and shortly before eleven o'clock the royal shooting brake which has been used for the transportation of luggage left Fort Belvedere, and also a dispatch rider

The Duke of Kent drove to Marlborough House shortly after 8 o'clock and at 10.15 a large car entered the gates with the Duke of York as its only passenger.

M.P.s warned to be at the House to-day; Mrs. Simpson's drive.—Page 3.

KING EDWARD VIII

DIARY OF THE DAY'S EVENTS

Noon.—Mr. Walter Monckton, K.C., Attorney-General to the Duchy of Cornwall, and Sir E. Peacock back at No. 10.

1.15 p.m.—Cabinet meeting ended.

3.33 p.m.—Mr Baldwin made his statement in Commons

4.5 p.m.—Duke of York arrived at Fort Belvedere.

5.0 p.m.—Queen Mary meets the King at Royal Lodge, Windsor Great Park.

9.0 p.m.—Duke of York arrives back at 145,

Piccadilly. The Prime Minister, Sir John Simon and Mr. Monckton at No. 10. Succession of messengers with brief cases.

9.15 p.m.—Mr. Malcolm MacDonald at No. 10.

10.0 p.m.—Sir John Simon and Mr. Monckton again at No. 10.

10.30 p.m.—Mr. Ramsay MacDonald at Colonial Office

11.20 p.m.—Mr. Monckton left No. 10 in the King's car.

Left: The Duke of Windsor & the lady he gave up the throne for, in exile in 1986.

Above: How the press reported the news of King Edward's abdication.

The Coronation of King George VI.
Inset: *The procession leaves Buckingham Palace.*
Main picture: *The State Coach passes through Admiralty Arch.*

Above: *The Royal Family on the balcony of Buckingham Palace after the Coronation.*

Top left: *King George VI receives the Jewelled Sword from the Archbishop of Canterbury.*

Top right: *King George VI holding the Sceptre with Dove and the Sceptre with Cross at his Coronation.*

essentially quiet and shy Prince Albert would find kingship a heavy burden to bear.

But the outgoing King Edward believed that his younger brother, so ably supported by Princess Elizabeth, would be more than a match for the job in hand.

In his abdication speech, and with an obvious sense of envy, he said of him: "He has one matchless blessing ... not bestowed on me, a happy home with his wife and children."

For her part Princess Elizabeth accepted her new role as Queen Consort (meaning she was not part of the constitution) with all her customary dignity and poise. These qualities - perceived as they were by the great British public - were to help the monarchy through its most difficult crisis in years.

In the space of thirteen years she had risen, quite unexpectedly, from virtual anonymity to a place beside her

husband on the throne of England. And the fortune-teller's prediction of twenty-six years earlier had come uncannily true!

Her daughters, too, were astonished by all that was happening around them. When the 11-year-old Princess Elizabeth saw a letter to 'H.M. The Queen' she realised with awe that it was addressed to her mother.

In February the family moved out of 145 Piccadilly and into the cavernous spaces of Buckingham Palace with its high ceilings, long corridors and austere formal rooms. In the coming months the new Queen would endeavour to turn it into a more comfortable home.

The Coronation of King George VI and Queen Elizabeth took place at Westminster Abbey, on Wednesday, May 12, 1937. The public, still reeling from the abdication shock, eagerly anticipated the event. They were not disappointed.

Thousands of people lined the route of the procession from Buckingham Palace to the Abbey, while millions more listened to a rather formal commentary on the radio.

The King and Queen rode in the famous Golden Coach pulled by eight grey horses and attended by a small army of liverymen.

Despite a few mishaps, the Coronation itself was an impressive ceremony. It was conducted by the Archbishop of Canterbury, attended by visiting dignitaries from all over the world - and lasted for several hours.

Afterwards the patiently waiting crowds cheered the newly-crowned royal couple all the way back to the palace.

The King and Queen, together with other members of the royal family, made several appearances on the palace balcony and not even the falling rain could quell the rapturous applause from below.

Later that evening, King George VI broadcast to the nation, the first time such a broadcast had ever been made.

It was the beginning of a new era for the British royal family.

King George VI and Queen Eizabeth visit Stratford-Upon-Avon, 1950.

Queen Consort

Queen Elizabeth, the Queen Consort, had lost her voice during the Coronation ceremony. But the very next day she was accompanying her husband on a tour of the East End of London. They were enthusiastically welcomed there with typical cockney good humour.

Later, they travelled all over Britain and always met with the same warmth from their loyal subjects.

The royal couple were also a great hit when they visited Paris in 1938. Although the journey was touched by sadness since it closely followed the death of Queen Elizabeth's mother.

The famous dress designer, Norman Hartnell, had produced a dazzling collection of dresses for the Queen to wear on the trip. However, since she was still in mourning it was felt that the clothes would be unsuitable.

In a flash of genius, Hartnell pointed out that it was a royal prerogative to wear white in mourning. The palace agreed and in the two weeks prior to the visit each of the dresses was remade in pure white. The result was an astonishing success in the fashion capital of the world. "We have taken the Queen to our hearts. She rules over two nations," reported one French newspaper.

On the final day of the visit, the King and Queen attended a concert at Versailles. At one point the music was completely drowned out by the roar of a fly-past of French Air Force fighter planes, an event which had been delayed earlier in the day.

The royal couple were both disturbed by the interruption. Unfortunately, it was a portent of things to come.

As the 1930's drew to a close, the clouds of conflict were darkening over Europe. Despite the strenuous efforts of British Prime Minister Neville Chamberlain, war with Germany seemed inevitable.

In May 1939, with the political situation worsening, King George VI and Queen Elizabeth reluctantly boarded the liner Empress of Australia for a scheduled tour of Canada and the USA.

The voyage across the Atlantic was horrendous with fog slowing the progress of the ship, so that the royals lost two days of their tour.

Left: *Princess Elizabeth undergoes training in the Auxilary Territorial Service.*

Main picture: *A Royal visit to one of the many blitzed areas in London.*

Just like the French before them, the Canadians and the Americans were bowled over by the charm of Queen Elizabeth. 'She smiled like an angel', said one newspaper headline.

The success of the tour did wonders for the confidence of the King and Queen.

Later, Queen Elizabeth said: "It made us, the King and I". It also helped to bring Britain and the United States closer together - a union which would prove more than valuable as history unfolded during the next five and a half years.

On July 22, the King, the Queen and their two daughters visited the Royal Naval College in Dartmouth. An 18-year-old Cadet Captain was detailed to entertain the two princesses. His name was Prince Philip of Greece. It was the beginning of a fine romance between the dashing young officer and Princess Elizabeth.

Less than two months later - at 11am on Sunday, September 3, 1939 - Great Britain declared war on Adolf Hitler's Germany.

At six o'clock that evening, King George broadcast to the nation: "In this grave hour, perhaps the most fateful in our history," he said, "I send to every household of my peoples, both at home and overseas, this message ... For the sake of all that we ourselves hold dear and of the world's order and peace it is unthinkable that we should refuse to meet this challenge ... To this high purpose, I now call my people at home and across the seas. I ask them to stand firm and united in this time of trial..." It was a stirring message.

A few days later, Queen Elizabeth broadcast a message to the women of the Commonwealth in which she touched the hearts of all the mothers who had recently seen their children evacuated. "The King and I know what it means to be parted from our children," she said.

Indeed, the two princesses spent the early months of the war in the comparative safety of Birkhall in Scotland. In December they moved to Sandringham in Norfolk, but were to spend most of the war in Windsor Castle.

The King and Queen remained at Buckingham Palace, determined to be close to the people of London.

Naturally, the knowledge that the royal couple were willing to share the dangers of the Blitz with the people, did a great deal for the nation's morale.

One night in September 1940, the King and Queen were lucky to escape unharmed when a bomb struck Buckingham Palace. They were both shaken by the blast, but stepped calmly out

Princess Elizabeth & the Duke of Edinburgh acknowledge the cheers of the crowd on the balcony of Buckingham Palace after their wedding in 1947.

of the wreckage. "I'm glad we've been bombed," said the Queen. "It makes me feel I can look the East End in the face".

Throughout the war, the royal couple visited many Blitzed areas as well as hospitals, air-raid shelters, fire stations and first-aid posts all over the country. And they were given a resounding, heartfelt welcome wherever they went.

Prime Minister Winston Churchill, whose own efforts at raising the fighting spirit of the British people were formidable indeed, wrote to them: "...Your Majesties are more beloved by all classes and conditions than any of the princes of the past," he said.

By the end of the war, in 1945,

King George VI had proved himself a worthy, brave and dedicated ruler. With his loyal and charming wife and his two fine children by his side, he had effectively erased the shocking effects of his brother's abdication and had restored the monarchy to its rightful place in the hearts and minds of the British people.

On July 10, 1947 the Palace announced the engagement of Princess Elizabeth to Prince Philip, soon to be created Duke of Edinburgh.

The royal wedding took place at Westminster Abbey, on November 20, 1947. It was a glittering occasion and proved to be just the tonic that Britain needed after the long dark days of war.

King George and Queen Elizabeth celebrated their Silver Wedding anniversary on April 26, 1948 and, once again, the public showered them with affection as they rode in a state landau from Buckingham Palace to a celebratory service at St. Paul's Cathedral.

That evening they were driven through many of the bomb-damaged streets of London and later made several appearances on the balcony at Buckingham Palace.

The King and Queen became proud grandparents on November 14, 1948 when Princess Elizabeth gave birth to Prince Charles at Buckingham Palace.

Almost two years later on August 15, 1950, Princess Anne was born at Clarence House, the home of Princess Elizabeth and the Duke of Edinburgh.

The happy family was growing and the presence of two bright young grandchildren brought endless joy to the royal couple.

But there was also sadness in the air.

King George's health had been failing for some months. In 1949 he had undergone an operation to improve the circulation in his right leg and to allay fears that the leg might have to be amputated.

In May 1951 the King and Queen opened the impressive Festival of Britain, on the south bank of the river Thames. In August the family travelled to Balmoral where they celebrated Princess Margaret's twenty-first birthday. While there King George was again taken ill.

At first it was thought to be a case of influenza, but was later diagnosed as lung cancer.

In September the brave King underwent an operation for the removal of his left lung. He appeared to have pulled through the ordeal and was able to enjoy Christmas at Sandringham with his family.

On Tuesday, February 5, 1952, King George seemed to be in good health. He enjoyed several hours shooting at

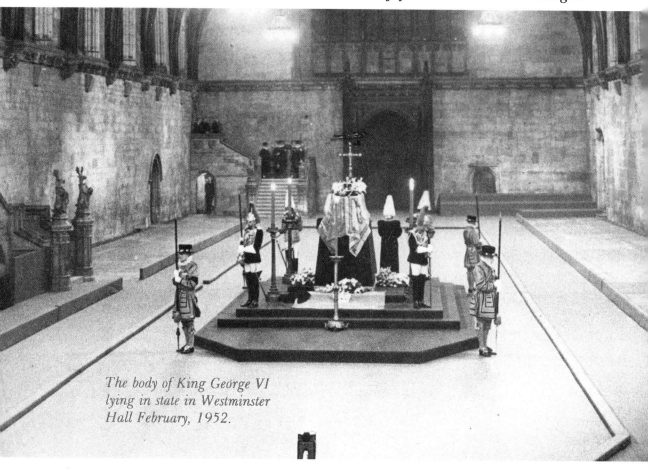

The body of King George VI lying in state in Westminster Hall February, 1952.

Sandringham where he was staying with Queen Elizabeth, Princess Margaret, Prince Charles and Princess Anne.

The King retired to bed and, sadly, was to die peacefully in his sleep during the early hours of February 6. He was succeeded by his eldest daughter who became Queen Elizabeth II.

At the time, the new Queen was travelling with Prince Philip in Africa. The young couple were at the famous Treetops Hotel in Kenya when they received the news of the King's death.

They returned home at once.

For four days King George VI's body lay in state inside London's Westminster Hall and over 300,000 people filed past to pay their last respects to a beloved monarch.

At 2pm on February 15, 1952, people all over the country observed two minutes silence in memory of the late King. This moving gesture was timed to coincide with the start of the funeral service at St. George's Chapel in Windsor.

The Queen Mother with the Dean of Windsor at the funeral of her husband.

The Queen Mother

Since 1952, Her Majesty Queen Elizabeth The Queen Mother, as she became known, has seen the arrivals of four more royal grandchildren - Prince Andrew, Prince Edward, Viscount Linley and Lady Sarah Armstrong-Jones.

She has enjoyed the weddings of Prince Charles, Princess Anne and Prince Andrew and the subsequent arrivals of her great-grandchildren - Peter and Zara Phillips, Prince William, Prince Henry, Princess Beatrice and Princess Eugenie.

Over the years she has attended countless royal engagements all over the world.

Notable among these was the Coronation of Queen Elizabeth II in June 1953, and the Investiture of the Prince of Wales at Caernarfon Castle in July 1969.

The Queen Mother has also maintained her interests in several walks of life. She has, for instance, amassed a notable collection of paintings, including works by Sickert, Nolan, Nash, Sisley and Lowry. And she has often enjoyed fly-fishing in a Scottish river.

In her youth, she has been a keen horsewoman and is now one of Britain's most successful race horse owners.

Perhaps her best-known horse was Devon Loch who has gone down in racing lore for a race lost! It was the 1956 Grand National in which Devon Loch was ridden by Dick Francis (now a famous thriller writer).

Coming into the home stretch ahead of the field the royal racer appeared to 'jump' an invisible fence before collapsing with all four legs splayed out. The

no man was more full of compassion ... He loved you all ... that was the pledge he took at the moment of his Coronation fifteen years ago. Now I am left alone, to do what I can to honour that pledge without him ... My only wish now is that I may be allowed to continue the work that we sought to do together."

Thirty-eight years after making that statement, there is no doubt that the Queen Mother has continued to honour the King's pledge and that she loves the British people is beyond doubt.

And the compliment is returned - for the British people adore her.

It has long been a tradition that on each succeeding August 4 people have gathered outside Clarence House to wish the Queen Mother a happy birthday.

This summer, as Her Majesty approaches her ninetieth year, the celebrations have begun earlier than usual. The nation can't wait to wish the Queen Mother many happy returns.

And the great lady herself has even expressed a wish that she will receive a telegram from the Queen in ten years time. Now that will be another great party to look forward to!

Happy birthday, Ma'am.

unusual accident allowed the 100-7 outsider ESB to take the race.

A long succession of Welsh corgis, too, have figured largely in the Queen Mother's life. Many of them were descended from the Queen's favourite, Susan, who was quite a character in royal circles during the 1950's.

In a statement to the nation in 1952, the Queen Mother said of her late husband: "... No man had a deeper sense than he of duty and service, and